4/95

D0015900

Also by Sandra Cisneros

FICTION

Woman Hollering Creek and Other Stories

The House on Mango Street

POETRY

My Wicked Wicked Ways

Loose Woman

Loose Woman

Poems by

Sandra Cisneros

Alfred A. Knopf New York 1994

THIS IS A BORZOI BOOK
PUBLISHED BY ALFRED A. KNOPF, INC.

Some of the poems in this work were originally published in the following:

Bomb Magazine: "I'm on My Way to Oklahoma to Bury the Man I Nearly Left My
Husband For," "Cloud," and "Black Lace Bra Kind of Woman" • *New York Times*
(Op/Ed section): "Little Clown, My Heart" • *Stone Drum Magazine*: "Why I Didn't"
• "Original Sin" and "Jumping off Roofs" were published in *Emergency Tacos*,
MARCH/ABRAZO Press • "Las Girlfriends" was published in *Intertext/Interstice: Chicanas
and Latinas on the Border*, Third Woman Press • "Down There" was published in *The
Sexuality of Latinas*, Third Woman Press.

Library of Congress Cataloging-in-Publication Data

Cisneros, Sandra.
    Loose woman / Sandra Cisneros. — 1st ed.
        p.   cm.
    ISBN 0-679-41644-7
    1. Women—United States—Poetry. 2. Love poetry, American.
I. Title.
PS3553.I78L66 1994
811'.54—dc20   93-35937
        CIP

Manufactured in the United States of America

First Edition

For Jasna,
as if our lives depended on it

"Life is life."

Contents

XXX

Acknowledgments

ᚷᚷ

There is no such thing as coincidences. I wish to thank the Lannan Foundation whose generosity arrived on a day of doubt and serious grief. I am grateful for its kind support and faith that yanked me back to art and sensibility. Here are the poems from that labor.

Eyes: Dennis Mathis, Drew Allen. *Ojos:* Norma Cantú. *Voces:* Sonia Saldívar Hull, Tey Diana Rebolledo, Ellie Hernández.

Corazón: En memoria de Danny López Lozano. These lives also left and were recorded in my heart—Astor Piazzolla, César Chávez, Cantinflas.

Las Madrinas: Susan Bergholz and Robin Desser, who poked under the bed with a broom and coaxed these poems to light.

Espíritu: Finally, I wish to thank Julie Grau, my editor at Turtle Bay, whose love and labor on my behalf allowed me to share my poetry.

To each, my heartfelt thanks.

Little Clown,
My Heart

Little Clown, My Heart

XXX

Little clown, my heart,
Spangled again and lopsided,
Handstands and Peking pirouettes,
Backflips snapping open like
A carpenter's hinged ruler,

Little gimp-footed hurray,
Paper parasol of pleasures,
Fleshy undertongue of sorrows,
Sweet potato plant of my addictions,

Acapulco cliff-diver *corazón*,
Fine as an obsidian dagger,
Alley-oop and here we go
Into the froth, my life,
Into the flames!

You Bring Out the Mexican in Me

✕✕

You bring out the Mexican in me.
The hunkered thick dark spiral.
The core of a heart howl.
The bitter bile.
The tequila *lágrimas* on Saturday all
through next weekend Sunday.
You are the one I'd let go the other loves for,
surrender my one-woman house.
Allow you red wine in bed,
even with my vintage lace linens.
Maybe. Maybe.

For you.

You bring out the Dolores del Río in me.
The Mexican spitfire in me.
The raw *navajas*, glint and passion in me.
The raise Cain and dance with the rooster-footed devil in me.
The spangled sequin in me.
The eagle and serpent in me.
The *mariachi* trumpets of the blood in me.
The Aztec love of war in me.
The fierce obsidian of the tongue in me.
The *berrinchuda, bien-cabrona* in me.
The Pandora's curiosity in me.
The pre-Columbian death and destruction in me.
The rainforest disaster, nuclear threat in me.

The fear of fascists in me.
Yes, you do. Yes, you do.

You bring out the colonizer in me.
The holocaust of desire in me.
The Mexico City '85 earthquake in me.
The Popocatepetl/Ixtaccíhuatl in me.
The tidal wave of recession in me.
The Agustín Lara hopeless romantic in me.
The *barbacoa taquitos* on Sunday in me.
The cover the mirrors with cloth in me.

Sweet twin. My wicked other,
I am the memory that circles your bed nights,
that tugs you taut as moon tugs ocean.
I claim you all mine,
arrogant as Manifest Destiny.
I want to rattle and rent you in two.
I want to defile you and raise hell.
I want to pull out the kitchen knives,
dull and sharp, and whisk the air with crosses.
Me sacas lo mexicana en mi,
like it or not, honey.

You bring out the Uled-Nayl in me.
The stand-back-white-bitch in me.
The switchblade in the boot in me.

The Acapulco cliff diver in me.
The *Flecha Roja* mountain disaster in me.
The *dengue* fever in me.
The *¡Alarma!* murderess in me.
I could kill in the name of you and think
it worth it. Brandish a fork and terrorize rivals,
female and male, who loiter and look at you,
languid in your light. Oh,

I am evil. I am the filth goddess Tlazoltéotl.
I am the swallower of sins.
The lust goddess without guilt.
The delicious debauchery. You bring out
the primordial exquisiteness in me.
The nasty obsession in me.
The corporal and venial sin in me.
The original transgression in me.

Red ocher. Yellow ocher. Indigo. Cochineal.
Piñón. Copal. Sweetgrass. Myrrh.
All you saints, blessed and terrible,
Virgen de Guadalupe, diosa Coatlicue,
I invoke you.

Quiero ser tuya. Only yours. Only you.
Quiero amarte. Atarte. Amarrarte.
Love the way a Mexican woman loves. Let
me show you. Love the only way I know how.

Original Sin

ᗢᗢ

Before Mexicana flight #729
en route to Mexico City departs
from San Antonio International Airport
I buy a 69¢ disposable razor at
the gift shop because I forgot
in Mexico they don't like hair
under your arms only on
your legs and plan to

shave before landing but
the stewardess handing out declaration
forms has given me the wrong
one assuming I'm Mexican but I am!
and I have to run up the aisle and ask
for a U.S. citizen form instead because
I'm well how do I explain?

except before you know it we're
already crossing the volcanoes and
descending into the valley of Mexico City
and I have to rush to the back
while the plane drops too quickly as
if the pilot's in a hurry to get home

and into the little airplane bathroom where
lots of couples want to coitus fantisizus but

I only want to get rid of my underarm hair
quick before the plane touches down in
the land of *los nopales* disregarding
lights blinking kindly return to your
seat and fasten your seatbelt all
in Spanish of course just in time

for flight #729 to deposit me finally
into the arms of awaiting Mexican kin
on my father's side of the family where
I open my arms wide armpits clean
as a newborn's soul without original
sin and embrace them like the good
girl my father would have
them believe I am.

Old Maids

ᴂ

My cousins and I,
we don't marry.
We're *too old*
by Mexican standards.

And the relatives
have long suspected
we can't anymore
in white.

My cousins and I,
we're all old
maids at thirty.

Who won't
dress children,
and *never*
saints—
though
we undress them.

The aunts,
they've given up on us.
No longer nudge—*You're next.*

Instead—
What happened in your childhood?

What left you all mean teens?
Who hurt you, honey?

But we've studied
marriages too long—

Aunt Ariadne,
Tía Vashti,
Comadre Penelope,
querida Malintzín,
Señora Pumpkin Shell—

lessons that served us well.

I Let Him Take Me

XX

I let him take me
over the threshold and over
the knee. I served and followed,
harbored up my things
and pilgrimed with him.
They snickered at my choice
when he took over
and I
vigiled that
solitude,
my life.
I labored love,
fierce stitched
and fed him.
Bedded and wifed him.
He never disappointed,
hurt, abandoned.
Husband, love, my life—
poem.

Extreme Unction

XX

I would've liked
to live with one
before
I turned complete.
That one I
could have desired
like a
prohibited
sweet.

Wonder now how
I would've
bellyed
his child.
Romanced
enough

I was
to believe
I could brave
that Ypres,
that Verdun.

Husband.
Balm for the occasional
itch. But I'm witch now.
Wife makes me wince.
My seamed tongue,
my eye blistered,
raise stink. And love
needs a smudged wink,
I think.

A Few Items to Consider

∞

First there is the scent of barley
to remember. Barley and rain.
The smooth terrain to recollect and savor.

Unforgiving whiteness of the room.
Ambiguity of linen. Purity.
Mute and still as photographs on the moon.

Everything here must be analyzed.
Catalogued. Studied twice.
A painstaking arrangement, almost vain.

Brandy glass with its one amber eye
on the bedside table. Shirt
draped across the chair. Woolen
trousers folded neatly in a square.
Little clock repeating—
precise, precise.

Not a stray whisker.
No comb full of dead hair.
No cup filled with coins and cuff

links and fingernail clippers.
A scrupulous chess game.
Formal. Concise.

There is much to learn.
Grace of the neck to memorize.
Heliotrope of sleep.
Hieroglyph of bones to decipher.
Love, if at all, comes later.

For now, the hands take to their dialogue.
Gullible as foreigners.
A greedy chattering, endlessly on nothing.
Nothing at all.

I Am So in Love I Grow a New Hymen

∞

Terrorists of the last
decade. Anarchists who fled
with my heart thudding on the back
bumper of a flatbed truck.
Nelson Algren impersonators.
Joe Hill detonators. *Los-más-
chingones-de-los-más-chingones-*
politically-correct-Marxist-tourists/voyeurs.
Olympic gold, silver, bronze love-
triathlons and several blue-
ribbon runner-ups to boot.
Forgot, forgotten, forget.
Past tense and no regrets.

No doubt you're Villa
and I'm Pershing's dizzy troops.
No doubt I'm eucalyptus and you
a California conflagration. No doubt
you're eucharist, Euclidean geometry,
World War II's Gibraltar strait,

the Chinese traders of Guangzhou,
Zapatistas breakfasting at Sanborn's,
Sassoferrato's cobalt blue,
Museo Poldi Pezzoli's insurance rate,
Gaudí's hammer against porcelain plates.

Ay, daddy, daddy, I
don't give a good goddamn. I
don't give
a good
god
damn.

Your Name Is Mine

XXX

And holy to me And your spirit
And that twin of divine
Death granted me in my sex
A complete breath And this silence
I trust And howl This body this

Spirit you give me
A gift of Taxco rain
Fine as silver
An antique pleasure
Obsidian and jade
The centuries I knew you

Even before I knew your man
Sex mother me The elegance
Of your jaguar mouth

Something Like Rivers Ran

⋙

undid the knot the ribbons
   the silk flags of motion
unraveled from under

the flesh of the wrists
   the stone of the lungs
something like water

broke free the prayer
   of the heart
the grief of the hands

crooned sweet when
   you held me
dissolved knee into knee

belly into belly
   an alphabet of limbs
ran urgently

nudged loose a pebble
   a pearl
a noose undoing its greed

and we were Buddha
and we were Jesus
and we were Allah

at once
a Ganges absolving
language woman man

You My Saltwater Pearl

〜

You my saltwater pearl,
my mother, my father,
my bastard child,
heaven and hurt,
you my slavery of sadness,
my wrinkled heart.

Little coin of my eye,
my tulip, my tin cup,
my woman, my boy,
to keep and be kept by,
to rankle and rile.

Take me like a boy,
hurt me a little. Make me cry.
I'm your milk and honey.
Your Nebuchadnezzar.
Your ziggurat of pleasure.
Your thumbprint of grief.

I'll be hashish.
The put aside not-for-sale
item for the maharaja,

vulgar as a Liz Taylor jewel.
Your Taj Mahal.

Please me. I'll pet you,
terrorize and take you.
Mother of my heart,
bastard child,
sweet mama, sweet daddy,
my saltwater pearl.

You Like to Give and Watch Me My Pleasure

ꝏ

You like to give and watch me my
pleasure. Machete me in two.
Take for the taking what is yours.
This is how you like to have me.

I'm as naked as a field of cane,
as alone as all of Cuba
before you.

You could descend like rain,
destroy like fire
if you chose to.

If you chose to.

I could rise like *huracán*.
I could erupt as sudden as
a coup d'état of trumpets,
the sleepless eye of ocean,

a sky of black *urracas*.
If I chose to.

I don't choose to.
I let myself be taken.

This power is my gift to you.

Christt You Delight Me

XXX

Christ you delight me,
Woolen scent of your sex,
Fury of your memory,
My hands still on the hilt
Of that excalibur of hip,
Blessed resurrection of thigh,
All these miles, *ay!*

Even now, as far away from you
As desert and mesa will allow,
Even now, under this welcome
Rain, yellow roses and honey-

Suckle vines, I have to hunker
My cunt close to the earth,
This little pendulum of mine
Ringing, ringing, ringing.

En Route to My Lover I Am Detained
by Too Many Cities and Human Frailty

XXX

Damn these damn
hours between me,
you. Cities and deserts
and hours and hours that widen
like dreams. And dreams that narrow
like bridges. And seconds
endless as all of Texas
lethargic and thick
under the dogday heat.

Hurry.
What matters is to be
inside the prayer of your body,
beneath the wings of your eyes,
the *chuparrosa* hummingbird being
in the man flower of your
sex.

Dulzura

✕✕

Make love to me in Spanish.
Not with that other tongue.
I want you *juntito a mí,*
tender like the language
crooned to babies.
I want to be that
lullabied, *mi bien*
querido, that loved.

I want you inside
the mouth of my heart,
inside the harp of my wrists,
the sweet meat of the mango,
in the gold that dangles
from my ears and neck.

Say my name. Say it.
The way it's supposed to be said.
I want to know that I knew you
even before I knew you.

You Called Me *Corazón*

XX

That was enough
for me to forgive you.
To spirit a tiger
from its cell.

Called me *corazón*
in that instant before
I let go the phone
back to its cradle.

Your voice small.
Heat of your eyes,
how I would've placed
my mouth on each.

Said *corazón*
and the word blazed
like a branch of *jacaranda*.

Love Poem for a Non-Believer

XX

Because I miss
you I run my hand
along the flat of my thigh
curve of the hip
mango of the ass Imagine
it your hand across
the thrum of ribs
arpeggio of the breasts
collarbones you adore
that I don't

My neck is thin
You could cup
it with one hand
Yank the life from me
if you wanted

I've cut my hair
You can't tug
my hair anymore
A jet of black
through the fingers now

Your hands cool
along the jaw

skin of the eyelids
nape of the neck
soft as a mouth

And when we open like apple
split each other in half and
have seen the heart
of the heart
of the heart that part
you don't I don't
show anyone the part
we want to reel

back as soon as it
is suddenly unreeled like silk
flag or the prayer call
of a Mohammed we won't
have a word for this except
perhaps religion

The Heart
Rounds Up
the Usual
Suspects

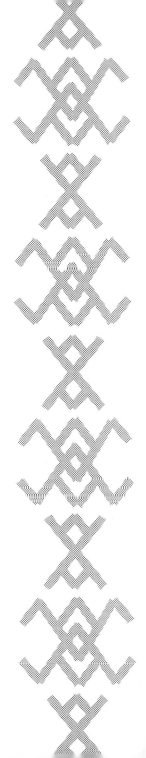

The Heart Rounds Up the Usual Suspects

XX

I sleep with the cat
when no one will have me.
When I can't give it away
for love or money—

I telephone the ones
who used to love me.
Or try to lure the leery
into my pretty web.

I'm loony as a June bride.
Cold as a *bruja's* tit.
A pathetic bitch.
In short, an ordinary woman.
Grateful to excessiveness.

At the slightest tug of generousness,
I stick to the cyclop who takes me,
lets me pee on the carpet
and keeps me fed.

Have you seen this woman?
I am considered harmless.
Armed and dangerous.
But only to me.

Waiting for a Lover

XX

And what if you don't arrive?
And what if you do?
I'm so afraid
I cross my fingers,
make a wish,
spit.

You're new.
You can't hurt me yet.
I light the candles.
Say my prayers.
Scent myself with mangoes.

I like the possibility of anything,
the little fear I feel
when you enter a room.
I haven't a clue of the who of you.

And what if you do like me?
And what if you do?
I can't think.
Dress myself in slinky black,

my 14-karat hoops and my velvet spikes.
Smoke two cigars.
I'm doing loopity loops.

Listen—cars roar by. All night.
I'm waiting for the one that stops.
All my life. Listen—
Hear that?
Yikes.

Well, If You Insist

XXX

My body, this
body, that has
nothing to do
with who
I am. But
it's my body,
this body you
long for. Sinew

and twist of flesh,
helix of desire and vanity.

These bodies. Your body.

My body. Ours
swallowing each other
whole. This. That.
Neck. Mouth. Cock. Cunt.

Little terrorist, you terrify me.
Come in then. Climb on. Get in.

Well, if you insist. If you
insist . . .

Pumpkin Eater

 ✕✕✕

I'm no trouble.
Honest to God I'm not.
I'm not

the kind of woman
who telephones in the middle of the night,
—who told you that?—
splitting the night like machete.
Before and after. After. Before.
No, no, not me.
I'm not

the she who slings words bigger than rocks,
sharper than Houdini knives,
verbal Molotovs.
The one who did that—*yo no fui*—
that wasn't me.

I'm no hysteric,
terrorist,
emotional anarchist.

I keep inside a pumpkin shell.
There I do very well.

Shut a blind eye to where
my pumpkin-eater roams.

I keep like fruitcake.
Subsist on air.
Not a worry nor care.
Please.
I'm as free for the taking
as the eyes of Saint Lucy.
No trouble at all.

I swear, I swear, I swear . . .

I Am So Depressed I Feel Like Jumping in the River Behind My House but Won't Because I'm Thirty-Eight and Not Eighteen

XX

Bring me a drink.
I need to think a little.
Paper. Pen.
And I could use the stink
of a good cigar—even
though the sun's out.
The grackles in the trees.
The grackles inside my heart.
Broken feathers and stiff wings.

I could jump.
But I don't.
You could kill me.
But you won't.

The grackles
calling to each other.
The long hours.
The long hours.
The long hours.

Bay Poem from Berkeley

XXX

Mornings I still
reach for you before
opening my eyes.

An antique habit from
last summer when we pulled
each other into the heat of groin
and belly, slept with an arm
around the other.

The Texas sun was like that.
Like a body asleep beside you.

But when I open my eyes
to the flannel and down,
mist at the window and blue
light from the bay, I remember
where I am.

This weight
on the other side of the bed
is only books, not you. What
I said I loved more than you.
True.

Though these mornings
I wish books loved back.

After Everything

〰〰〰

It's always the same.
No liquor in the house.
The last cigar snuffed in its ashes.
And a heavy dose of poems.

At two a.m. you know
that can't be good for you.
But there I go,
arteries crackling like
artillery when I dial.

East or west.
Central or Pacific.
Chicago, San Antonio, New York.

And when I'm through
hurling words as big as stones,
slashing the air with my tongue,
detonating wives and
setting babies crying.

And when my lovers are finished
telling me—You're nuts,

Go screw yourself,
Stop yelling and speak English please!

After everything
that's breakable is broken,
the silence expensive,
the dial tone howling like my heart.

I Want to Be a Father Like the Men

XXX

I want to be a father
like the men
I've loved.

Each with their
little starfish
beside them.
Their bold Arctic flag.
Their tug of affirmation
who fright me with the eye
and bone and jaw
I recognize and thought
I claimed as mine.

I'd like to give
without disgrace
my name.
To search for he, for she

who is my own to keep
exclusively.
To neither
give away nor loan.

I want to know
how love can grow irrevocable
and prove the fable true.

A love exists that gives.

And won't take back what's given.
Like the men.

El Alacrán Güero

XXX

They say *el alacrán güero* can kill
you. That's what they say.
Of all the scorpions that exist,
the white one is the deadliest.

One sting
makes the tongue thick,
asphyxiates.
Before you know it,
you are another
femme fatality.

Beware *el alacrán güero*
whose grief arrives delayed.

Even if all your life
you'd been warned.
Even if you'd snuffed
your eyes to their beauty
like a passionate Saint Lucy.
You are not immune.

Unaware is how Death
will find you. Coiled
in your righteous sleep.

Shake the sheets.
Stand the bed in cans of water.
Look before you leap.

Beware *el alacrán güero,*
I tell you.
I know of what I speak.

Thing in My Shoe

XX

Thing in my shoe,
dandelion, thorn, thumbprint,
one grain of grief that has me undone once more,
oh my father, heartily sorry am I for this right-side of the brain
who has alarmed and maimed and laid me many a day now
    invalid low.
I should know, I'm full of its decibel.
This me that is me that is mine all mine
under one and twenty eiderdowns.
I confess

a certain foppy sappiness regular as the 26-day flow,
like the macabre Carlotta. Under duress
I sprout like the potato in its greedy gloom.
Yowl like the black cat howling with its rowdy need.
Shut up! What I want is to be

saved like the lucky fuck
when the gypsies arrive in the nick,

their *bandoneónes* and violins
releasing the prisoners of the brain's Bastille!

Why not? I'm for emotions running amok tonight,
breaking china and getting fucked.
I'm a regular Notre Dame, I tell you.
Little braindoors and gargoyled gutters,
and the frothy mob with their machetes and clubs
wild about me, I tell you,
positively screaming blood.

Night Madness Poem

XX

There's a poem in my head
like too many cups of coffee.
A pea under twenty eiderdowns.
A sadness in my heart like stone.
A telephone. And always my
night madness that outs like bats
across this Texas sky.

I'm the crazy lady they warned you about.
The she of rumor talked about—
and worse, who talks.

It's no secret.
I'm here. Under a circle of light.
The light always on, resisting a glass,
an easy cigar. The kind

who reels the twilight sky.
Swoop circling.
I'm witch woman high
on tobacco and holy water.

I'm a woman delighted with her disasters.
They give me something to do.
A profession of sorts.

Keeps me industrious
and of some serviceable use.

In dreams the origami of the brain
opens like a fist, a pomegranate,
an expensive geometry.

Not true.
I haven't a clue
why I'm rumpled tonight.

Choose your weapon.
Mine—the telephone, my tongue.
Both black as a gun.

I have the magic of words,
the power to charm and kill at will.
To kill myself or to aim haphazardly.
And kill you.

I Don't Like Being in Love

꧁

Not like this. Not tonight,
a white stone. When you're 36
and seething like sixteen
next to the telephone,
and you don't know where.
And worse—with whom?

I don't care for this fruit. This
Mexican love hidden in the boot.
This knotted braid. Birthcord buried
beneath the knuckle of the heart.

Cat at the window scratching at
the windswept moon
scurrying along, scurrying along.
Trees rattling. Screen
doors banging raspy.

Brain a whorl of swirling
fish. Oh, not like this.
Not this.

Amorcito Corazón

XXX

Ya no eres
mi amorcito
¿verdad?

Ya lo supe.
Ya lo sé.

Fuiste
y ya no eres.
Fuimos
y se acabó.

¿Cómo les diría?
¿Cómo se explica?

Te conocí
¿y ahora?

no.

A Little Grief Like Gouache

✗✗✗

Without a ping
Or pang or knuckle rap or
Notion

Tobacco-stained
How do you do
Thrum without a name

Droopy as a sunflower
Delinquent as a god
Full of riotous ache and goofy

A Van Gogh ocher
Drizzled did and giddy
Left me
Light-tippled dizzy
Fled

Full Moon and You're Not Here

XXX

Useless moon,
too beautiful to waste.
But you, my Cinderella,
have the midnight curfew,
a son waiting to be picked up from his den meeting,
and the fractured marriage weighing on your head
like a crown of thorns.

Oh my beauty,
it's not polite
to keep me waiting.
To send me reeling into a spiral
and then to say good night.

I smoke a cigar,
play a tango,
gulp my gin and tonic.

Goddamn you.

Full moon and you're not here.
I take off the silk slip,
the silver bangles.

You're in love with my mind.

But sometimes, sweetheart,
a woman needs a man
who loves her ass.

My Friend Turns Beautiful Before My Eyes

ⅩⅩ

Sir Walter Raleigh,
dimity and damask,
rococo and arabesque,
batiste and challis,
handkerchief and crumpled glove.

Love, I don't know
how you suddenly grew lovely,
why I never noticed last
summer, nor the summers before
when the hard sun died
anything before it bloomed.

My seasonal lovers have come and gone.
And you were there, friend,
cold as porcelain,
mute as the milk moon.
I was afraid of you then.

Did you notice
I never hovered
in the cab of your pickup
when we good-byed,
when the pecan trees
rustled and shushed.

A pink lantern burning
patient on my porch.
Nipped kiss. Screen door
slammed. I danced
barefoot with the cat

when I was alone.
Glass of wine,
candle, my brush
across my hair a hundred
times. And now,

here you are.
Little asterisk, little
How-I-wonder-what-you-are
upon my linen.

Incest! Error!
My head split in two—
half of me preening its feathers,
the other watching from
a stool and sneering—
Fool!

Perras

XXX

I can't imagine that goofy white woman
with you. Her pink skin on your dark.
Your tongue on hers. I can't
imagine without laughing.
Who would've thought.

Not her ex-boyfriend—
your good ol' ex-favorite best buddy,
the one you swore was thicker than kin,
blood white brother, friend—
who wants to slit you open like a pig
and I don't blame him.

Isn't it funny.
He acting Mexican.
You acting white.

I can't imagine this woman.
Nor your white ex-wife. Nor any
of those you've hugged and held,
so foreign from the country we shared.

Damn. Where's your respect?
You could've used a little imagination.
Picked someone I didn't know. Or at least,
a bitch more to my liking.

Unos Cuantos Piquetitos

XXX

Here—the bull
's eye of my heart,
snappy red
flag against bone
white page.

Here, that electrical
cord—my jugular.
Looking forward to the
guillotine precision.

Here, the easy wrists.
Quick, neat, convenient.

For your comic amusement,
that Dodo, my womb,
pinched from disuse.

And here, gentlemen, ladies!
mis palabras.

With Lorenzo at the Center of the Universe, el Zócalo, Mexico City

XX

We had to cross the street twice
because of rats. But there it was.
The *zócalo* at night and *la Calle de la Moneda*
like a dream out of Canaletto. Forget
Canaletto. This was real.

And you were there, Lorenzo.
The cathedral smoky-eyed and still
rising like a pyramid after all
these centuries. You named the four
holy centers—Amecameca, Tepeyac, and two
others I can't remember. I remember you,
querida flecha, and how all the words I knew
left me. The ones in English and the few
in Spanish too.

This is the center of the universe,
I said and meant it. This is eternity.
This moment. Now. And love,
that wisp of copal that scared the hell
out of you when I mentioned it,
love is eternal, though
what eternity has to do with tomorrow,
I don't know. Understand?

I'm not sure you followed me.
Not now, not then. But I know
what I felt when I put my hand

on your heart, and there was that kiss,
just that, from the center of the universe.
Or at least my universe.

Lorenzo, is the center of the universe
always so lonely at night and so
crowded in the day? Earlier
I'd been birthed from the earth
when the metro bust loose at noon.
Stumbled up the steps over Bic pens
embroidered with Batman logos, red
extension cords, vinyl wallets, velveteen
roses, pumpkin seed vendors, brilliant
masons looking for work. I remember the boy
with the burnt foot carried by his mother,
the smell of meat frying, a Styrofoam
plate sticky with grease.

At night we fled
the racket of Garibaldi and *mariachi*
chasing cars down *Avenida Lázaro Cárdenas*
for their next meal. At *La Hermosa Hortensia*,
lights bright as an ice cream parlor,
faces sweaty and creased with grief.
My first pulque warm and frothy like semen.

On the last evening we said good-bye
along two streets named after rivers. I

fumbled with the story of Borges and his Delia.
When we meet again beside what river?
But this was no poem. Only mosquitoes
biting like hell and a good-bye
kiss like a mosquito bite that left
me mad for hours. After all,
hadn't it taken centuries for us
to meet at the center of the universe
and consummate a kiss?

Lorenzo, I forget what's real.
I mix up the details of what happened
with what I witnessed inside my
universe. Is it like that for you?
But I thought for a moment, I really did,
that a kiss could be a universe.
Or sex. Or love, that old shoe. See.
Still hopeless. Still writing poems
for pretty men. Half of me alive
again. The other shouting from the sidelines,
Sit down, clown.

Ah, Lorenzo, I'm a fool.
Eternity or bust. That's how it is with me.
Even if eternity is simply one kiss,

one night, one moment. And if love isn't
eternal, what's the point?

If I knew the words I'd explain
how a man loves a woman before love
and how he loves her after
is never the same. How the two halves split
and can't be put back whole again.
Isn't it a shame?

You named the holy centers but forgot
one—the heart. Said every
time you'd pass this *zócalo*
you'd think of me and that kiss
from the center of the universe.

I remember you, Lorenzo. See
this *zócalo?* Remember me.

I Awake in the Middle of the Night
and Wonder If You've Been Taken

XX

At any moment, the soldiers could arrive.
At any given second, Sarajevo could surrender.
One could give up as well the nuisance of surviving.

At any moment, a precise second might claim you.
At any decisive point, God might not give a damn.
You're there, in that city. You don't count. You're not history.

In my own bed of down and vintage linen,
beside an altar of Buddhas and Madres Dolorosas
and lace and Storyville mirrors,
I'm here. Awake from the bad dream.

I'm a woman like you.
I don't count either.
Not a thing I say.
Not a thing I do.

Small Madness

XX

I swear, I will not
let go to these
small madnesses
at two a.m. I will not
be manic as a
Marilyn Monroe
seeking her savior-
executioner. I will not
love like heroin,
be martyr of extreme self-
inflicted grief, nor
romance myself into a
tired *"Fin."*

This I swear this near
year of my life's end,
my life dangling,
a live wire, some
fierce and likely
trick, a Mexico City fire-
eater's deep and desperate
breath. I swear,
life of mine, thick as a
foreign coin, beautiful
as money and as brutal,

you are my first allegiance.
I have no other lover.
I press my mouth to yours,
my faithful wife-beater,
and stifle this *mariachi*
howl.

Heart,
My Lovely
Hobo

Heart, My Lovely Hobo

XXX

Heart, my lovely hobo, you
remember, then, that afternoon in Venice
when all the pigeons rose flooding the piazza
like a vaulted ceiling. That was you
and you alone who grinned.

Fat as an oyster,
pulpy as a plum,
raw, exposed, naive,
dumb. As if love
could be curbed, and grace
could save you from the daily beatings.

Those blue jewels of flowers in the arbor
that the bees loved. Oh, there'll be other
flowers, a cat maybe beside the bougainvillea,
a little boat with flags glittering in the harbor
to make you laugh,
to make you spiral once more.
Not this throbbing.
This.

I Am on My Way to Oklahoma to Bury the Man
I Nearly Left My Husband For

XX

Your name doesn't matter.
I loved you.
We loved.
The years

       I waited
by the river for your pickup
truck to find me. Footprints
scattered in the yellow sand.
Husband, mother-
in-law, kids wondering
where I'd gone.

         You wouldn't
the years I begged. Would
the years I wouldn't. Only
one of us had sense at a time.

I won't see you again.

I guess life presents you
choices and you choose. Smarter
over the years. Oh smarter.
The sensible thing smarting

over the years, the sensible
thing to excess, I guess.

My life—deed I have
done to artistic extreme—I
drag you with me. Must wake
early. Ride north tomorrow.
Send you off. Are you fine?
I think of you often, friend,
and fondly.

Cloud

> If you are a poet, you will see clearly that there is a cloud
> floating in this sheet of paper.
>
> —*Thich Nhat Hanh*

ⵉⵉⵉ

Before you became a cloud, you were an ocean, roiled and
murmuring like a mouth. You were the shadow of a cloud cross-
ing over a field of tulips. You were the tears of a man who cried
into a plaid handkerchief. You were a sky without a hat. Your
heart puffed and flowered like sheets drying on a line.

And when you were a tree, you listened to trees and the tree
things trees told you. You were the wind in the wheels of a red
bicycle. You were the spidery *María* tattooed on the hairless arm
of a boy in downtown Houston. You were the rain rolling off the
waxy leaves of a magnolia tree. A lock of straw-colored hair
wedged between the mottled pages of a Victor Hugo novel. A
crescent of soap. A spider the color of a fingernail. The black nets
beneath the sea of olive trees. A skein of blue wool. A tea saucer
wrapped in newspaper. An empty cracker tin. A bowl of blueber-
ries in heavy cream. White wine in a green-stemmed glass.

And when you opened your wings to wind, across the punched-
tin sky above a prison courtyard, those condemned to death and
those condemned to life watched how smooth and sweet a white
cloud glides.

Tú Que Sabes de Amor

for Ito Romo

XXX

You come from that country
where the bitter is more bitter
and the sweet, sweeter.

You come from that town split
down the center like a cleft lip.
You come from the world
with a river running through it.
The dead. The living.
The river Styx.

You come from the twin Laredos.
Where the world was twice-named and
nopalitos flower like a ripe *ranchera.*
Ay, corazón, ¿tú que sabes de amor?

No wonder your heart is filled
with *mil peso* notes and *jacaranda.*
No wonder the clouds laugh each
time they cross without papers.

I know who you are.
You come from that country
where the bitter is more bitter
and the sweet, sweeter.

Once Again I Prove the Theory of Relativity

XX

If
you came back
I'd treat you
like a lost Matisse
couch you like a Pasha
dance a Sevillana
leap and backflip like a Taiwanese diva
bang cymbals like a Chinese opera
roar like a Fellini soundtrack
and laugh like the little dog that
watched the cow jump over the moon

I'd be your clown
I'd tell you funny stories and
paint clouds on the walls of my house
dress the bed in its best linen
And while you slept
I'd hold my breath and watch
you move like a sunflower

How beautiful you are
like the color inside an ear
like a conch shell
like a Modigliani nude

I'll cut a bit of your hair this time
so that you'll never leave me
Ah, the softest hair
Ah, the softest

If
you came back
I'd give you parrot tulips and papayas
laugh at your stories
Or I wouldn't say a word which,
as you know, is hard for me

I know when you grew tired
off you'd go to Patagonia
Cairo Istanbul
Katmandu
Laredo

Meanwhile
I'll have savored you like an oyster
memorized you
held you under my tongue
learned you by heart
So that when you leave
I'll write poems

Fan of a Floating Woman

after Shikibu

XX

Your morning
glories are beautiful
to look at in this photograph.
Beautiful is how I remember them.

And I think a man who grows morning glories
because he loves their beautifulness, must be a beautiful man.
Here. I want to make a gift of this fan. Write my name on it for you
to place in this man's house of yours. Perhaps to stake I've been here.

Only a fan. Not a glass shoe. Not a pomegranate seed. Not a coffee
cup or key. You'll smooth the sheets. Punch the bruised pillows
when I'm gone. It will be as it was before. *Mundo sin fin.*
The silences again tugged taut as linen.

Perhaps another will pluck this fan with
its clatter of courtrooms and pianos.
Wonder who I am.

That Beautiful Boy
Who Lives Across from the Handy Andy

XXX

invited me
to his birthday
party. Twenty-
eight this Saturday,
December 2nd, 1989.
So Saturday

night I am going
to put on my prettiest
dress, the black one
with the green
and purple sequins,
and my cowboy boots.

And I am going
to be there
with a six-pack
and this poem,

like any fool who loves
to look at a cloud,
or evening poppy,
or a red red pickup truck.

for John Hernández in memoriam

Black Lace Bra Kind of Woman

for la Terry

ꟽ

¡Wáchale! She's a black lace bra
kind of woman, the kind who serves
up suicide with every kamikaze
poured in the neon blue of evening.
A tease and a twirl. I've seen that
two-step girl in action. I've gambled bad
odds and sat shotgun when she rambled
her '59 Pontiac between the blurred
lines dividing sense from senselessness.

Ruin your clothes, she will.
Get you home way after hours.
Drive her '59 seventy-five on 35
like there is no tomorrow.
Woman zydeco-ing into her own decade.
Thirty years pleated behind her like
the wail of a San Antonio accordion.
And now the good times are coming. Girl,
I tell you, the good times are here.

Down There

At that moment, Little Flower scratched herself
where one never scratches oneself.

from "The Smallest Woman in the World"
—Clarice Lispector

Your poem thinks it's *bad*.
Because it farts in the bath.
Cracks its knuckles in class.
Grabs its balls in public
and adjusts—one,
then the other—
back and forth like Slinky. No,
more like the motion
of a lava lamp.
You follow me?

Your poem thinks it
cool to pee in the pool.
Waits for the moment
someone's watching before
it sticks a finger up
its nose and licks
it. Your poem's weird.

The kind that swaggers in like Wayne
or struts its stuff like Rambo.
The kind that learned
to spit at 13 and still
is doing it.

It blames its bad habits
on the Catholic school.

Picked up words that
snapped like bra straps.
Learned words that ignite
of their own gas
like a butt hole flower.
Fell in love with words
that thudded like stones and sticks.
Or stung like fists.
Or stank like shit
gorillas throw at zoos.

Your poem never washes
its hands after using the can.
Stands around rolling
toilet paper into wet balls
it can toss up to the ceiling
just to watch them stick.
Yuk yuk.

Your poem is a used rubber
sticky on the floor
the next morning,

the black elephant
skin of the testicles,
hairy as kiwi fruit
and silly,

the shaving
stubble against the purity
of porcelain,

one black pubic
hair on the sexy
lip of toilet seat,

the swirl of spit
with a cream of celery
center,

a cigarette
stub sent hissing
to the piss pot,

half-finished
bottles of beer reeking
their yeast incense,

the miscellany of maleness:
nail clippers and keys,
tobacco and ashes,
pennies quarters nickels dimes and
dollars folded into complicated origami,
stub of ticket and pencil and cigarette, and
the crumb of the pockets

all scattered on the Irish
linen of the bedside table.

Oh my little booger,
it's true.

Because someone once
said Don't
do that!
you like to do it.

Baby, I'd like to mention
the Tampax you pulled with your teeth
once in a *Playboy* poem*
and found it, darling, not so bloody.
Not so bloody at all, in fact.
Hardly blood cousin
except for an unfortunate
association of color
that makes you want to swoon.

Yes,
I want to talk at length about Men-
struation. Or my period.

*John Updike's "Cunts" in *Playboy* (January 1984), 163.

Or the rag as you so lovingly put it.
All right then.

I'd like to mention my rag time.

Gelatinous. Steamy
and lovely to the light to look at
like a good glass of burgundy. Suddenly
I'm artist each month.
The star inside this like a ruby.
Fascinating bits of sticky
I-don't-know-what-stuff.
The afterbirth without the birth.
The gobs of a strawberry jam.
Membrane stretchy like
saliva in your hand.

It's important you feel its slickness,
understand the texture isn't bloody at all.
That you don't gush
between the legs. Rather,
it unravels itself like string
from some deep deep center—
like a Russian subatomic submarine,
or better, like a mad Karlov cackling

behind beakers and blooping spirals.
Still with me?

Oh I know, darling,
I'm indulging, but indulge
me if you please.
I find the subject charming.

In fact,
I'd like to dab my fingers
in my inkwell
and write a poem across the wall.
"A Poem of Womanhood"
Now wouldn't that be something?

Words writ in blood. But no,
not blood at all, I told you.
If blood is thicker than water, then
menstruation is thicker than brother-
hood. And the way

it metamorphosizes! Dazzles.
Changing daily
like starlight.
From the first

transparent drop of light
to the fifth day chocolate paste.

I haven't mentioned smell. Think
Persian rug.
But thicker. Think
cello.
But richer.
A sweet exotic snuff
from an ancient prehistoric center.
Dark, distinct,
and excellently
female.

Los Desnudos: A Triptych

XX

I

In this portrait of *The Naked Maja* by Goya
I'll replace that naughty *duquesa*
with a you. And you
will do nicely too, my maharaja.
The *gitano* curls and the skin a tone
darker than usual because
you've just returned from Campeche.
All the same, it's you raised
with your arms behind your head
staring coyly at me from the motel pillows.

Instead of the erotic breasts,
we'll have the male eggs to look at
and the pretty sex.
In detail will I labor the down
from belly to the fury of
pubis dark and sweet,
luxury of man-thigh
and coyness of my maja's eyes.

My velvet and ruffled eye will linger,
precise as brushstrokes,
take pleasure in the looking and look long.
This is how I would paint you.
In the leisure of your lounging.
Both nude and naked to my pleasure.

Let me look with greedy
eye and greedy appetite, my
petty mischief. Let me wonder
at your wordlessness. What
are you thinking when you look like that?
We do not belong one to the other
except now and again intermittently.
Of that infinity, freely
you give yourself to me to take
and I take freely.

II

This time my subject is
a man with the eyes
of a *nagual* or a Zapata.
But you can't see his eyes.
What you get a good view of is his famous backside.
He is painted à la Diego holding calla lilies
in the rich siennas and olives of a native.
He is the one with the sleepy gaze.
My favorite child and centerpiece.
I divulge this information because as favorite
I would like to take my time. But,
he belongs to another, and I own him
borrowed.

When Frida finds out she'll freak, all hell will break,
the telephone won't stop *fregando*.
How could a sister? How?
I'm not sister nor is love now
nor ever will be
politically correct.

I know an artist does what she must do,
and art is a jealous spouse.
You share me with my *husband*,
and I share you as well
with that *otra* you call wife.

My life, I don't mind.
You are a lovely calla.
I do not look to lure you from your life.
Don't think to pluck me to fidelity.
I love you. You love me.
We need this passion.

Agreed.

III

Like a Mexican Venus at his toilet,
I put you here with your back to me
and your flat Indian ass. *Ay,* beauty!
The little angel holding up the mirror
is me, of course, and me
refracted from this poem.

I love you languid like this, a vain
man, and leisurely I love the slim
limbs and slim bones. You're very
pretty primped and pretty proud as
any man is wont to be. You're eternally
mine to look at and paint as I see fit.

I can't quit
you though
time and time again
you quit me.
I can't quit the looking
though you and I are past
the time of epic wars. Wars

and love and love and wars
have disunited and united us.
All the same, I look back and looking back
I am reflected in that mirror,
you with your back to me,
me facing backwards. Little
one, I love

you. I can't forget you.
You can't forget me.
I won't let you.

Mexicans in France

ɣɣ

He says he likes Mexico.
Especially all that history.
That's what I understand
although my French
is not that good.

And wants to talk
about U.S. racism.
It's not often he meets
Mexicans in the south of France.

He remembers
a Mexican Marlon Brando once
on French tv.

How, in westerns,
the Mexicans are always
the bad guys. And—

Is it true
all Mexicans
carry knives?

I laugh.
—Lucky for you

I'm not carrying my knife
today.

He laughs too.
—I think
the knife you carry
is
abstract.

My Nemesis Arrives After a Long Hiatus

XXX

I

I paint my toes matador red.
Snap freshly dried sheets.
Pull taut. Tuck corners.
Wax floors. Rub mirrors.
Oil my body and sleep

under the midnoon eye.
While the thwack, thwack, thwack
of the carpenter's hammer
next door stops long enough
to watch me slip
into the pool. A man's hollow
laugh getting a load of my Indian ass.

I wash towels. Scent linen.
Stock fridge with things to eat.
Slice pineapple, melon, strawberries.
Inspect my body where the tan
line stops abrupt as a stand-
up comic. Silly belly soft as
the yolk of an egg.

I wash with soap made from Italian
honey. Wrap a clean towel
around my hair.
Perfume skin. Paint
lips into a perfect
bull's-eye.

Admire clouds,
how they travel with
the grace of snails.

When sun leaves, you'll come.

II

Crumpled pillow. Coffee cup.
Flaccid rubbers on the bedside table.
Chair askew. Breakfast jam on the carpet.
Cigarette crushed into a saucer.

From the road, your car—
that burgundy dollop
color of my menstruation—
leaving and leaving and leaving me.

III

My goddess Guadalupe is
more powerful than your god Marx.
Volviste—¿no?

Volverás.

IV

I light my bedroom with *faroles* and *papel picado*.
Paper lanterns, paper flags bought at the wooden
stands in front of the San Miguel Church
at Christmas. Tissue flags
from one beam to the next. Sleep
inside the triangle of that prayer.

Rose, tangerine, turquoise, jade,
Ave Maria blue. Sweet as an apricot,
soft as the silk fringe of my best shawl.
Mexican cutouts. Christmas *faroles*.
Bright as parasols, carnival, confetti.
You laughed, remember?

But that night.
Embroidered flowers, embroidered birds.

V

In the clatter of your departures,
I write poems.
Poems

the wind flutters.
Papel de China.
Paper flowers, paper wings.

A Man in My Bed Like Cracker Crumbs

XX

I've stripped the bed.
Shaken the sheets and slumped
those fat pillows like tired tongues
out the window for air and sun
to get to. I've let

the mattress lounge in
its blue-striped dressing gown.
I've punched and fluffed.
All morning. I've billowed and snapped.
Said my prayers to *la Virgen de la Soledad*
and now I can sit down
to my typewriter and cup
because she's answered me.

Coffee's good.
Dust motes somersault and spin.
House clean.
I'm alone again.
Amen.

Bienvenido Poem for Sophie

XXX

This morning that would've meant
a field of crumpled snow if we
were in Vermont, brought only
a crumpled sky to Texas,

and you and Alba for breakfast
tacos at Torres Taco Haven
where you admired my table
next to the jukebox and
said, Good place to write.

You promised we could come back
and have tacos together and sit
here with coffee and our writer's
notebooks whenever we want.
And nobody would have to talk
if we didn't want to. Next time

you come by my house, I want
to take you up to the roof.
At sunset the grackles
make a wonderful racket.
You can come whenever you want.
And nobody will have to talk
if we don't want to.

Arturito the Amazing Baby Olmec
Who Is Mine by Way of Water

XX

Arturito, when you were born
the hospital gasped when
they fished you from your fist of sleep,
a rude welcome you didn't like a bit,
and I don't blame you. The world's a mess.

You inherited the family sleepiness and overslept.
And in that sea the days were nacre.
When you arrived on Mexican time,
you were a wonder, a splendor, a plunder,
more royal than any Olmec
and as mysterious and grand.
And everyone said "*¡Ay!*"
or "Oh!" depending on their native tongue.

So, here you are, godchild,
a marvel that could compete with any ancient god
asleep beneath the Campeche corn. *A ti te tocó*
the aunt who dislikes kids and Catholics,
your godmother. Don't cry!
What do amazing godmothers do?
They give amazing gifts. Mine to you—
three wishes.

First, I wish you noble like Zapata,
because a man is one who guards

those weaker than himself.
Second, I wish you a Gandhi wisdom,
he knew power is not the fist,
he knew the power of the powerless.
Third, I wish you Mother Teresa generous.
Because the way of wealth is giving
yourself away to others.

Zapata, Gandhi, Mother Teresa.
Great plans! Grand joy! Amazingness!
For you, my godchild, nothing less.
These are my wishes, Arturo Olmec,
Arturito amazing boy.

Escribí este poema para mi ahijado, Arturo Javier Cisneros Zamora,
el 8 de febrero, 1993, en San Antonio de Bexar, Tejas.

Jumping off Roofs

✕✕✕

Bet your feet burned
when you landed.
That's for sure.

Only child playing with your only self.

First the chicken shed
in the corrugated Laredo heat.

Then the roof of the big
house when mama and the aunts
were all asleep.

And years later,
off a plane on some fool dare
you couldn't back out of.
So the story goes.

How your heart opened like silk.
The crooked spin of horizon.
That awful slant of sky.
And finally, the ripcord
and the yank

of life to bring you
back to earth.

Broke an ankle. Bone
split into a thousand colors.
Swell story to tell and tell again
at a San Antonio ice house.

But what I want to know is this.
In that dizzy moment
did your peepee dangle
like a ripcord,
or is it true all men
have hard-ons
when they fall to earth?

And if so,
what is the good
of being close to heaven
if our souls have business with the angels
but our peepees
so much to do with earth.

Why I Didn't

〤

Of course.
I was going to, you know.
Or maybe you didn't.

Already my mouth gone soft
when you kissed me good night
and let me go.

But instead of love
there was only an old sleeping bag
you tossed at me and three
flea bites on my belly
the next morning.
You didn't know *that*,
did you?

I didn't think so.

Nor your name I stole
and took with me
all the way from San Antonio
to Puerto Escondido.

And today when I waited

for your pickup to appear,
I'll be right back, and left me there
on your porch full of suitcases and
crates and saws and cedar,

I went into your room
and lay down on your bed
just to see if it'd suit me.
The sheets were cool
and a fine talc of dust lay everywhere
the way some men who live alone
are used to living.

Oh I'm scared all right.
Haven't you noticed, I'm
only shy when I like a man.
And to tell the truth
I'm not sure love is worth
the risk of losing friendship.

It would've been easy.
I could've claimed
I was afraid of the dark.
I am, you know. Afraid I mean.

But there was that plane
to catch the next morning.
And you had to go to work.

Besides, I was sleepy.
And love, that fish too old to get away,
will be there the next morning. And if not,
there are other mornings, other fish.

Las Girlfriends

XXX

Tip the barmaid in tight jeans.
She's my friend.
Been to hell and back again.
I've been there too.

Girlfriend, I believe in Gandhi.
But some nights nothing says it
quite precise like a Lone Star
cracked on someone's head.

Last week in this same bar,
kicked a cowboy in the butt
who made a grab for Terry's ass.
How do I explain, it was all
of Texas I was kicking,
and all our asses on the line.

At Tacoland, Cat flamencoing crazy
circles round the pool
player with the furry tongue.
A warpath of sorts for every
wrong ever wronged us.

And Terry here has her own history.
A bar down the street she can't

go in, and one downtown. Me,
a French café in Austin
where they don't say—*entrez-vous.*

Little Rose of San Antone
is the queen bee of kick-*nalga.*
When you go out with her,
don't wear your good clothes.

But the best story is la Bárbara
who runs for the biggest kitchen knife
in the house every bad-ass domestic quarrel.
Points it towards her own heart
like some Aztec priestess gone *loca.*
¡ME MATO!

I tell you, nights like these,
something bubbles from
the tips of our pointy boots
to the top of our coyote yowl.

Ya'll wicked mean, a voice at the bar
claims. Naw, not mean. Shit!
Been to hell and back again.
Girl, me too.

Champagne Poem for La Josie

for Josie Garza

XXX

The first glass will make you laugh.
The second will have you making others laugh.
The third is for singing operettas.
The fourth to give you wings.
The fifth will have you forget
the things you chose to remember
and remember things you chose to forget.
The sixth is for courage when dialing Him.
The seventh to bring down cuss and concupiscence.
Congratulations. The eighth will drive you to bed or brawl.
Or to brawl in bed. Same difference.

Still Life with Potatoes, Pearls, Raw Meat, Rhinestones, Lard, and Horse Hooves

for Franco Mondini

☒

In Spanish it's *naturaleza muerta* and not life at all.
But certainly not natural. What's natural?
You and me. I'll buy you a drink.
To a woman who doesn't act like a woman.
To a man who doesn't act like a man.
Death is natural, at least in Spanish, I think.
Life? I'm not so sure.
Consider The Contéssa, who in her time was lovely
and now sports a wart the size of this diamond.
So, *ragazzo*, you're Venice.
To you. To Venice.
Not the one of Casanova.
The other one of cheap pensiones by the railway station.
I recommend a narrow bed stained with semen, pee, and sorrow
    facing the wall.
Stain and decay are romantic.
You're positively Pasolini.
Likely to dangle and fandango yourself to death.
If we let you. I won't let you!
Not to be outdone I'm Piazzolla.
I'll tango for you in a lace G-string
stained with my first-day flow
and one sloppy tit leaping like a Niagara from my dress.
Did you say duress or dress?
Let's sing a Puccini duet—I like *La Traviesa.*
I'll be your trained monkey.
I'll be sequin and bangle.
I'll be Mae, Joan, Bette, Marlene for you—

I'll be anything you ask. But ask me something glamorous.
Only make me laugh.
Another?
What I want to say, *querido,* is
hunger is not romantic to the hungry.
What I want to say is
fear is not so thrilling if you're the one afraid.
What I want to say is
poverty's not quaint when it's your house you can't escape from.
Decay's not beautiful to the decayed.
What's beauty?
Lipstick on a penis.
A kiss on a running sore.
A reptile stiletto that could puncture a heart.
A brick through the windshield that means I love you.
A hurt that bangs on the door.
Look, I hate to break this to you, but this isn't Venice or Buenos
Aires.
This is San Antonio.
That mirror isn't a yard sale.
It's a fire. And these are remnants
of what could be carried out and saved.
The pearls? I bought them at the Winn's.
My mink? Genuine acrylic.
Thank God this isn't Berlin.
Another drink?
Bartender, another bottle, but—
¡Ay caray and oh dear!—

The pretty blond boy is no longer serving us.
To the death camps! To the death camps!
How rude! How vulgar!
Drink up, honey. I've got money.
Doesn't he know who we are?
Que vivan los de abajo de los de abajo,
los de rienda suelta, the witches, the women,
the dangerous, the queer.
Que vivan las perras.
"Que me sirvan otro trago . . ."
I know a bar where they'll buy us drinks
if I wear my skirt on my head and you come in wearing nothing
but my black brassiere.

Vino Tinto

✕✕✕

Dark wine reminds me of you.
The burgundies and cabernets.
The tang and thrum and hiss
that spiral like Egyptian silk,
blood bit from a lip, black
smoke from a cigarette.

Nights that swell like cork.
This night. A thousand.
Under a single lamplight.
In public or alone.
Very late or very early.
When I write my poems.

Something of you still taut
still tugs still pulls,
a rope that trembled
hummed between us.
Hummed, love, didn't it.
Love, how it hummed.

Loose Woman

XX

They say I'm a beast.
And feast on it. When all along
I thought that's what a woman was.

They say I'm a bitch.
Or witch. I've claimed
the same and never winced.

They say I'm a *macha*, hell on wheels,
viva-la-vulva, fire and brimstone,
man-hating, devastating,
boogey-woman lesbian.
Not necessarily,
but I like the compliment.

The mob arrives with stones and sticks
to maim and lame and do me in.
All the same, when I open my mouth,
they wobble like gin.

Diamonds and pearls
tumble from my tongue.

Or toads and serpents.
Depending on the mood I'm in.

I like the itch I provoke.
The rustle of rumor
like crinoline.

I am the woman of myth and bullshit.
(True. I authored some of it.)
I built my little house of ill repute.
Brick by brick. Labored,
loved and masoned it.

I live like so.
Heart as sail, ballast, rudder, bow.
Rowdy. Indulgent to excess.
My sin and success—
I think of me to gluttony.

By all accounts I am
a danger to society.
I'm Pancha Villa.

I break laws,
upset the natural order,
anguish the Pope and make fathers cry.
I am beyond the jaw of law.
I'm *la desperada*, most-wanted public enemy.
My happy picture grinning from the wall.

I strike terror among the men.
I can't be bothered what they think.
¡Que se vayan a la ching chang chong!
For this, the cross, the Calvary.
In other words, I'm anarchy.

I'm an aim-well,
shoot-sharp,
sharp-tongued,
sharp-thinking,
fast-speaking,
foot-loose,
loose-tongued,
let-loose,
woman-on-the-loose

loose woman.
Beware, honey.

I'm Bitch. Beast. *Macha.*
¡Wáchale!
Ping! Ping! Ping!
I break things.

A Note About the Author

Sandra Cisneros was born in Chicago on December 20, 1954, the third child in a family of seven children. The only daughter of a Mexican father and a Mexican-American mother, she was educated in the Midwest before moving to the Southwest in 1984. She has worked as a teacher of high-school dropouts, a poet-in-the-schools, a college recruiter, an arts administrator, and most recently as a visiting writer at a number of universities around the country. The recipient of numerous awards for her poetry and fiction, Cisneros is the author of *The House on Mango Street* (Arte Público Press, 1984/Vintage, 1991), *My Wicked Wicked Ways* (Third Woman, 1987/Turtle Bay, 1992), *Woman Hollering Creek and Other Stories* (Random House, 1991/Vintage, 1992), and *Loose Woman* (Knopf, 1993). Sandra Cisneros's books have been translated into ten languages. She makes her home in the borderlands—San Antonio, Texas—where she is currently at work on a novel.

A Note on the Type

This book has been set on the Macintosh in the Adobe version of Weiss, a typeface originally designed in Germany by Emil Rudolf Weiss (1875–1942). The design of the roman was completed in 1928 and that of the italic in 1931. Both are well-balanced and even in color, and both reflect the subtle skill of a fine calligrapher.

Printed and bound by Arcata/Fairfield, Fairfield, Pennsylvania
Designed by Virginia Tan